Wedding Planner
Checklist

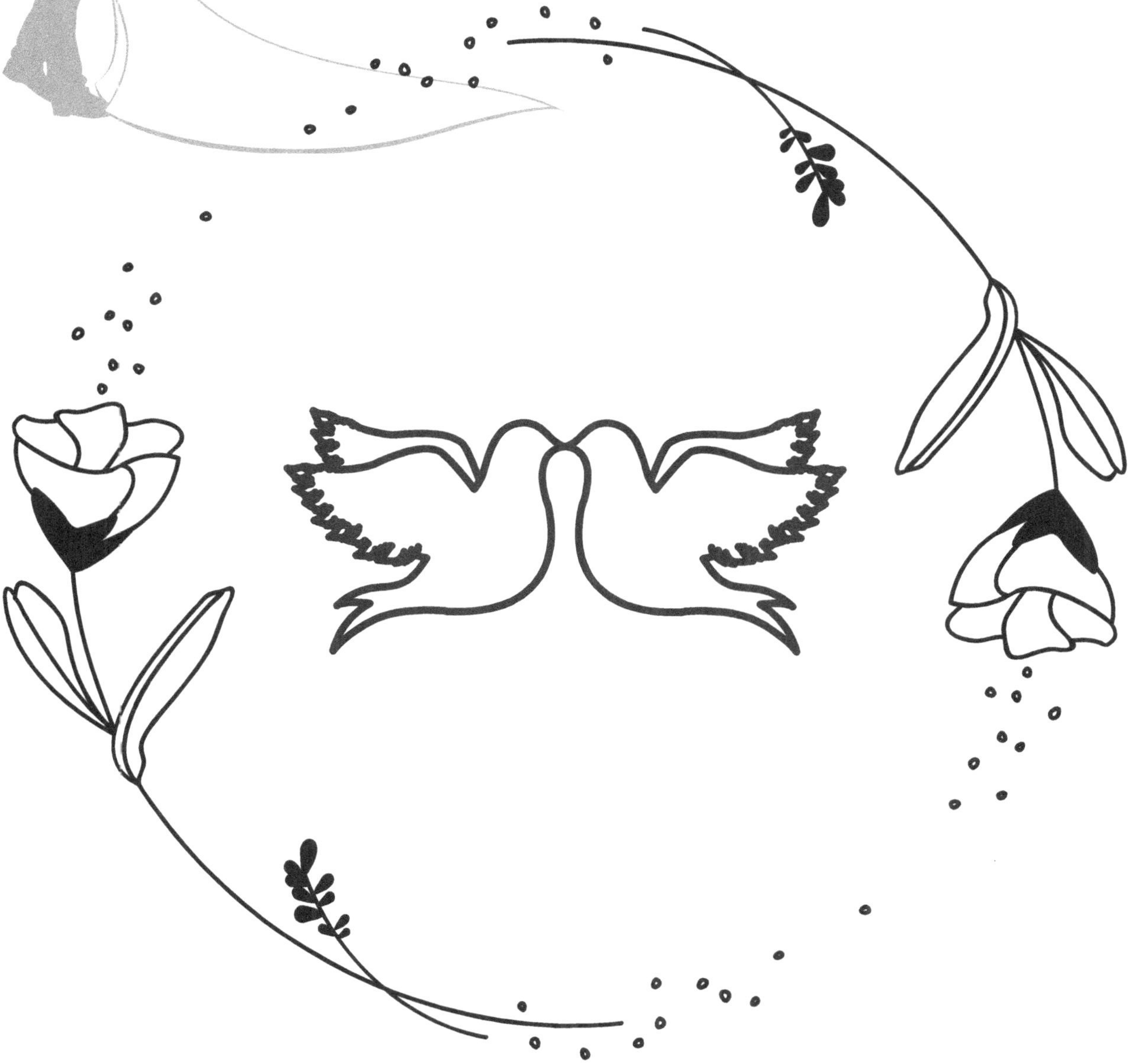

Wedding Planner

____

&

____

Wedding Date

Time:

Wedding Venue

Wedding Contact

● Wedding Planner

Name: ....   Phone: ....

Email: ....   Location: ....

Web: ....

● Reception Venue

Name: ....   Phone: ....

Email: ....   Location: ....

Web: ....

● Caterer

Name: ....   Phone: ....

Email: ....   Location: ....

Web: ....

● Ceremony Venue

Name: ....   Phone: ....

Email: ....   Location: ....

Web: ....

● Officiant

Name: ....   Phone: ....

Email: ....   Location: ....

Web: ....

● Photographer

Name: ....   Phone: ....

Email: ....   Location: ....

Web: ....

● Videographer

Name: ....   Phone: ....

Email: ....   Location: ....

Web: ....

● Florist

Name: ....   Phone: ....

Email: ....   Location: ....

Web: ....

Wedding Contact

● Shop / Dress Designer

Name: ....

Email: ....

Web: ....

Phone: ....

Location: ....

● Bridal Attier

Name: ....

Email: ....

Web: ....

Phone: ....

Location: ....

● Bridal Jewelry

Name: ....

Email: ....

Web: ....

Phone: ....

Location: ....

● Hair Stylist

Name: ....

Email: ....

Web: ....

Phone: ....

Location: ....

● Makeup Artist

Name: ....

Email: ....

Web: ....

Phone: ....

Location: ....

● Stationary Designer

Name: ....

Email: ....

Web: ....

Phone: ....

Location: ....

● DJ Party Entertainment

Name: ....

Email: ....

Web: ....

Phone: ....

Location: ....

● Honeymoon- Hotel/Resort

Name: ....

Email: ....

Web: ....

Phone: ....

Location: ....

Wedding Contact

● **Welcome Party Venue**

Name: ....   Phone: ....

Email: ....   Location: ....

Web: ....

◍ **Rehearsal Dinner Venue:**

Name: ....   Phone: ....

Email: ....   Location: ....

Web: ....

● **Wedding cake:**

Name: ....   Phone: ....

Email: ....   Location: ....

Web: ....

◍ **Other:**

Name: ....   Phone: ....

Email: ....   Location: ....

Web: ....

●

Name: ....   Phone: ....

Email: ....   Location: ....

Web: ....

◍

Name: ....   Phone: ....

Email: ....   Location: ....

Web: ....

●

Name: ....   Phone: ....

Email: ....   Location: ....

Web: ....

◍

Name: ....   Phone: ....

Email: ....   Location: ....

Web: ....

Important Date

Note

Date:

Date:

Date:

Date:

Date:

Date:

Date:

Date:

Date:

Date:

Date:

Date:

Date:

Date:

Date:

Important Date

Date:

Date:

Date:

Note

Date:

Date:

Date:

Date:

Date:

Date:

Date:

Date:

Date:

Date:

Date:

Date:

 # Wedding Budget 

Details	Cost	Deposit	Remainder

Note & Special Remainder: ....

Wedding Budget

Details	Cost	Deposit	Remainder

Note & Special Remainder: ....
....
....
....
....
....

Wedding Budget

Details	Cost	Deposit	Remainder

Note & Special Remainder: ....
....
....
....
....
....

Wedding Budget

Details	Cost	Deposit	Remainder

Note & Special Remainder:
....
....
....
....
....
....

Wedding Budget

Details	Cost	Deposit	Remainder

Note & Special Remainder: ....
....
....
....
....
....

Wedding Budget

Details	Cost	Deposit	Remainder

Note & Special Remainder: ....

 # Wedding Budget 

Details	Cost	Deposit	Remainder

Note & Special Remainder: ....
....
....
....
....
....

Wedding Budget

Details	Cost	Deposit	Remainder

Note & Special Remainder:
....
....
....
....
....
....

Wedding Budget

Details	Cost	Deposit	Remainder

Note & Special Remainder: ....
....
....
....
....
....

Wedding Budget

Details	Cost	Deposit	Remainder

Note & Special Remainder:

Ceremony Expense Tracker

Details	Budget	Cost	Deposit	Blance	Due Date
Officiant Gratuity					
Marriage License					
Venue Cost					
Flowers					
Decorations					

Note & Special Remainder:

Expense Snapshot
Reception Expense Tracker

Details	Budget	Cost	Deposit	Blance	Due Date
Venue Fee					
Catering					
Bar / Beverages					
Cake / Cutting Fee					
Decorations					
Rental					
Bartender Stuff					

Note & Special Remainder:

Checklist
12 Month Before

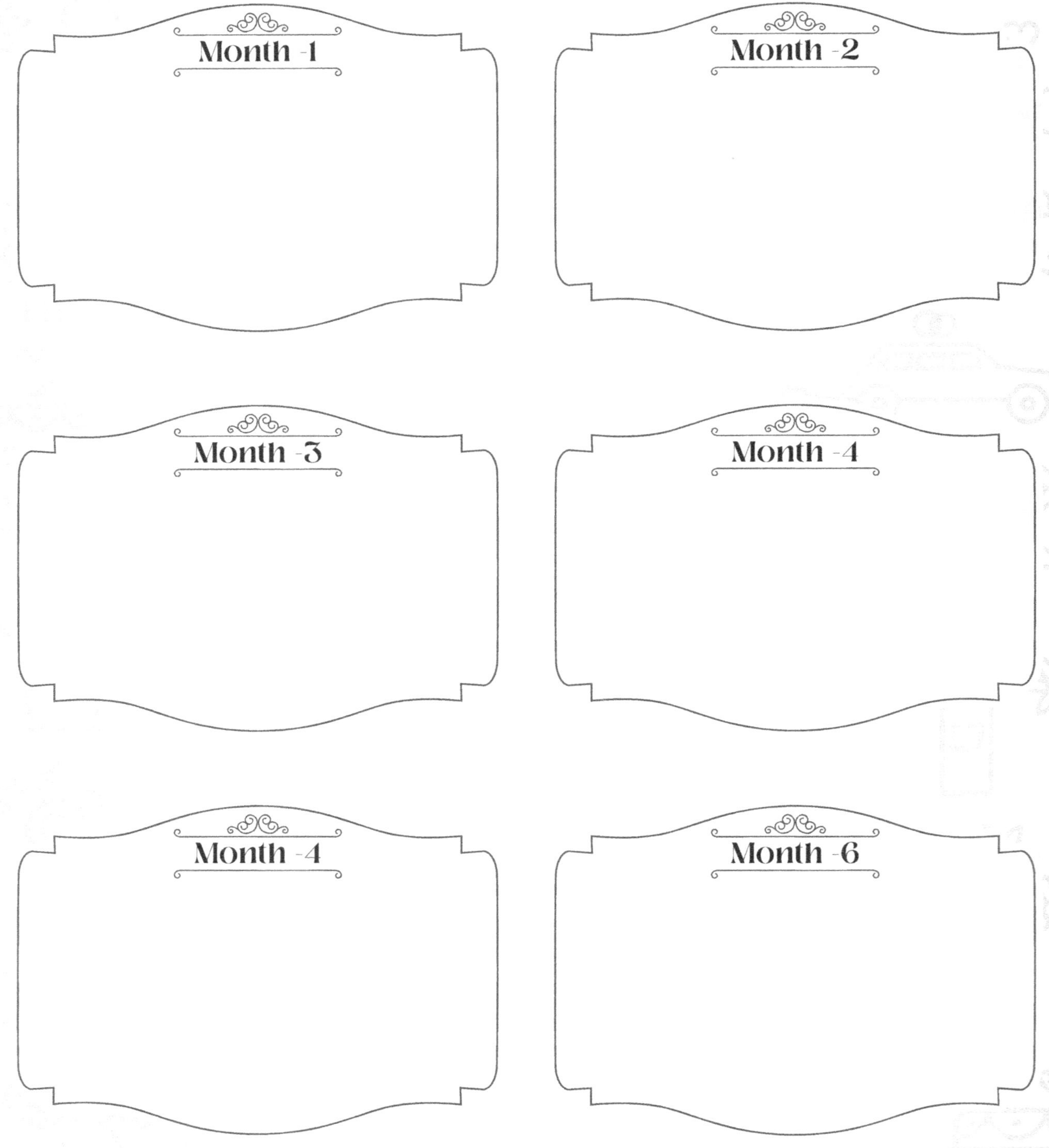

Checklist
12 Month Before

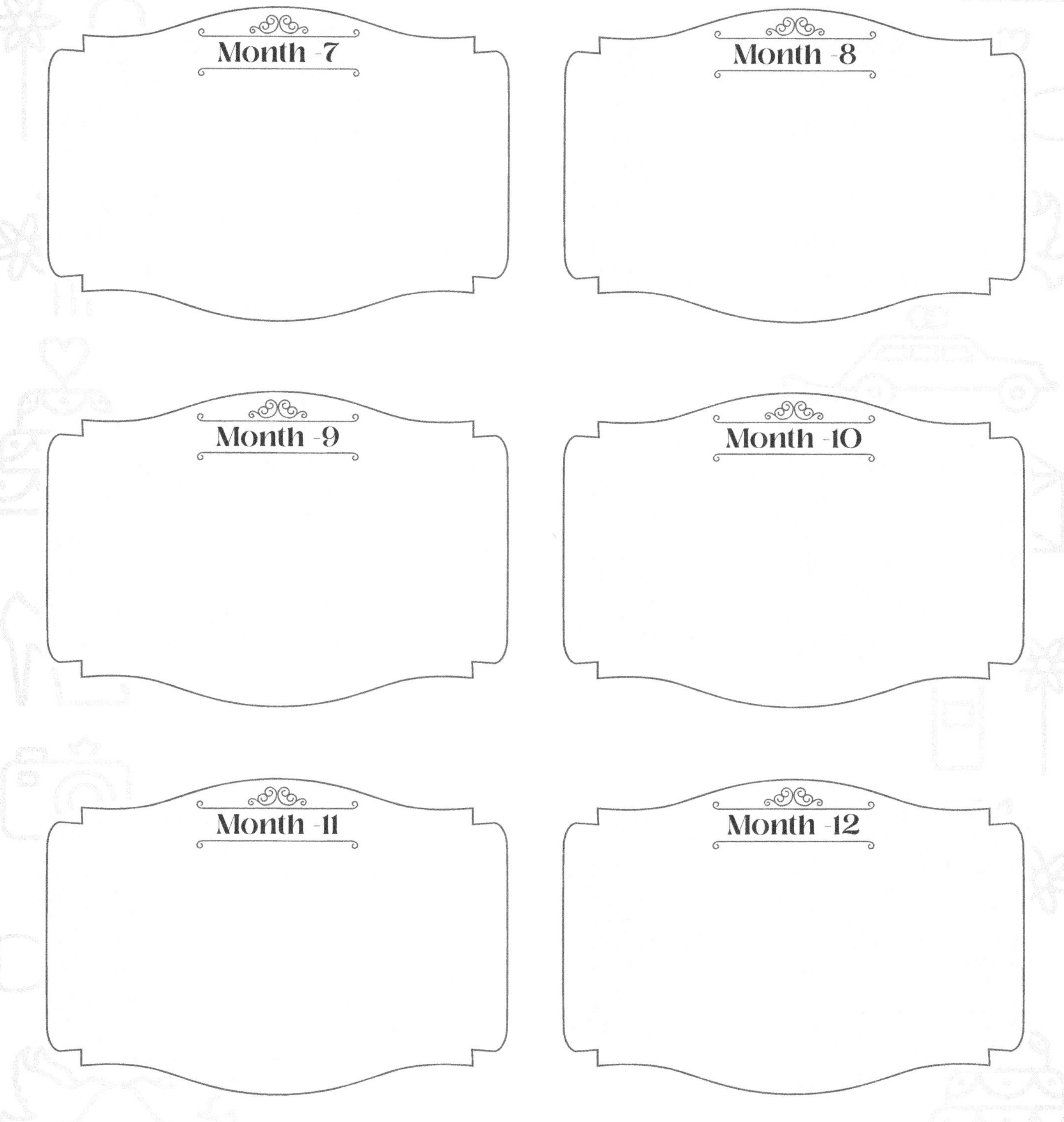

Guest List

Name	Phone	Email/Address

 # Guest List 

Name	Phone	Email/Address

Guest List

Name	Phone	Email/Address

Guest List

Name	Phone	Email/Address

Guest List

Name	Phone	Email/Address

Guest List

Name	Phone	Email/Address

Guest List

Name	Phone	Email/Address

Guest List

Name	Phone	Email/Address

Guest List

Name	Phone	Email/Address

Guest List

Name	Phone	Email/Address

Guest List

Name	Phone	Email/Address

 # Guest List 

Name	Phone	Email/Address

To Do List

Planning Notes

To Do List

Planning Notes

To Do List

Planning Notes

To Do List

Planning Notes

To Do List

Planning Notes

To Do List

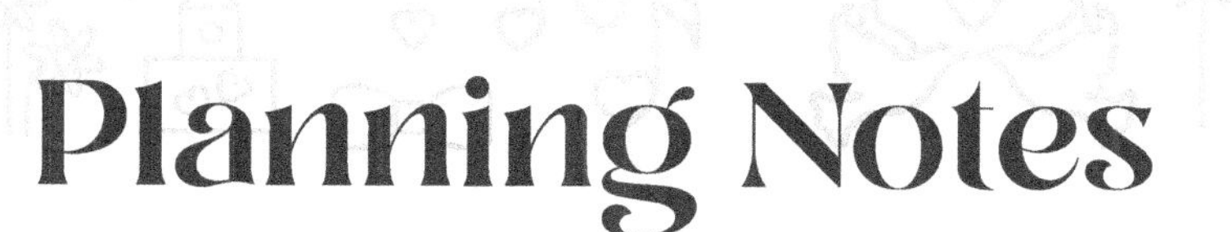

Planning Notes

To Do List

Planning Notes

To Do List

Planning Notes

To Do List

Planning Notes

To Do List

Planning Notes

To Do List

Planning Notes

To Do List

Planning Notes

To Do List

Planning Notes

To Do List

Planning Notes

To Do List

Planning Notes

To Do List

Planning Notes

To Do List

Planning Notes

To Do List

Planning Notes

To Do List

Planning Notes

To Do List

Planning Notes

To Do List

Planning Notes

To Do List

Planning Notes

To Do List

Planning Notes

To Do List

Planning Notes

To Do List

Planning Notes

To Do List

Planning Notes

To Do List

Planning Notes

To Do List

Planning Notes

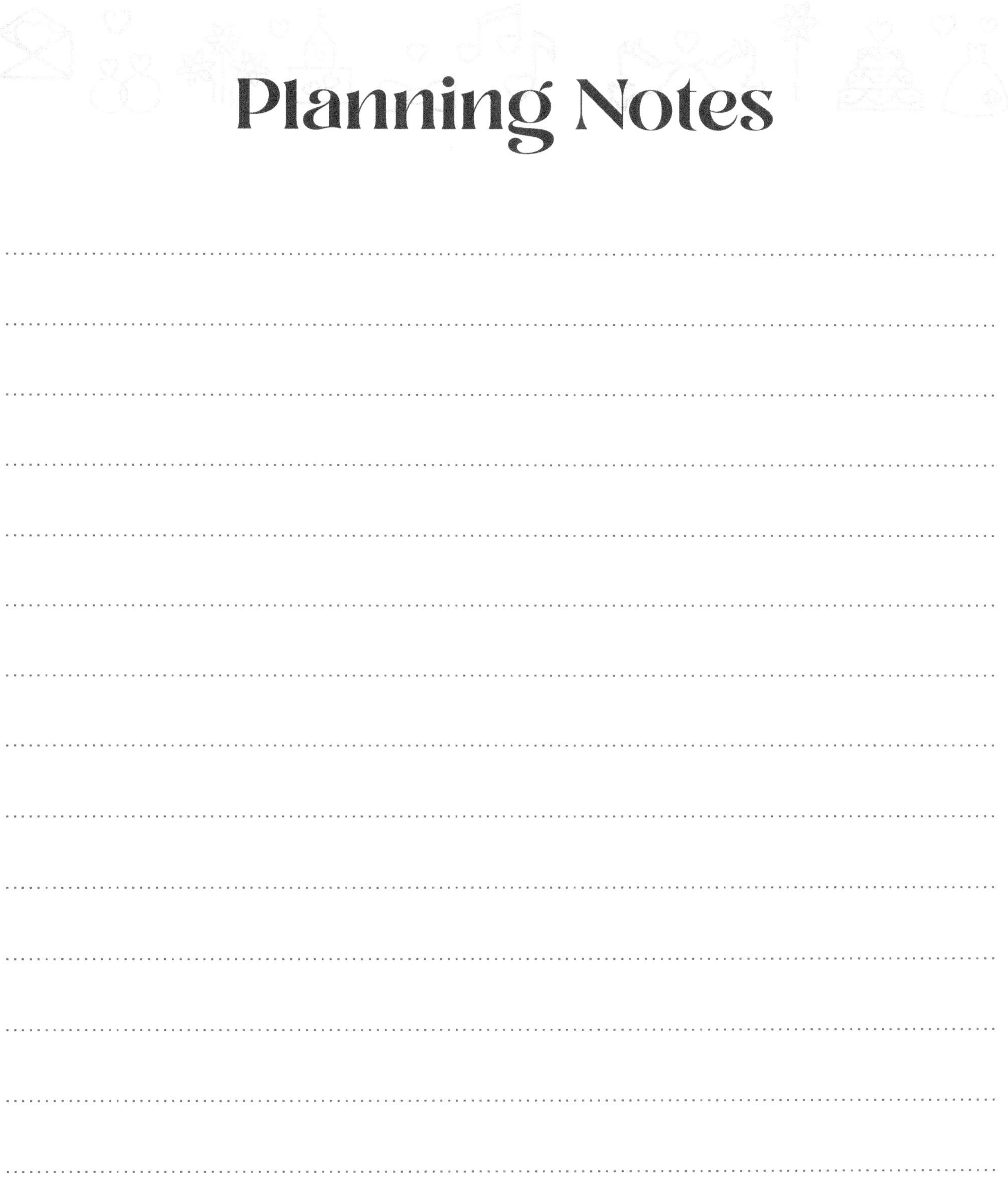

To Do List

Planning Notes

To Do List

Planning Notes

To Do List

Planning Notes

To Do List

Planning Notes

To Do List

Planning Notes

To Do List

Planning Notes

To Do List

Planning Notes

To Do List

Planning Notes

Gift List

Date	Gift Description	Given by	Thank Yo Send

Note & Special Remainder:
....
....
....
....
....

Gift List

Date	Gift Description	Given by	Thank Yo Send

Note & Special Remainder: ....

Gift List

Date	Gift Description	Given by	Thank Yo Send

Note & Special Remainder: ....

Gift List

Date	Gift Description	Given by	Thank Yo Send

Note & Special Remainder:

Gift List

Date	Gift Description	Given by	Thank Yo Send

Note & Special Remainder: ....

Gift List

Date	Gift Description	Given by	Thank Yo Send

Note & Special Remainder:

Gift List

Date	Gift Description	Given by	Thank Yo Send

Note & Special Remainder: ....
....
....
....
....

Gift List

Date	Gift Description	Given by	Thank Yo Send

Note & Special Remainder: ....
....
....
....
....
....

Gift List

Date	Gift Description	Given by	Thank Yo Send

Note & Special Remainder:

Gift List

Date	Gift Description	Given by	Thank Yo Send

Note & Special Remainder: ....
....
....
....
....
....

Gift List

Date	Gift Description	Given by	Thank Yo Send

Note & Special Remainder: ....
....
....
....
....
....

"A successful marriage
is an edifice that must be
rebuilt every day"

- Andre Maurois-

Hey there!!!

We hope you enjoyed our book. As a small family company, your feedback is very important to us. Please let us know how you like our book at:

believepublisher@gmail.com

Without your voice we don't exist!

Please, support us and leave a review!

Thank you!!!

www.ingramcontent.com/pod-product-compliance
Lightning Source LLC
LaVergne TN
LVHW060559200726
843509LV00003B/157